FEELING GOOD

Raising self-esteem in the primary school classroom

Noreen Wetton
AND
Peter Cansell

FORBES PUBLICATIONS

FEELING GOOD

To Jill, who made it possible
To many children, in many places
Illustrations by Jill Cansell

Inigo House, 29 Bedford Street, London WC2E 9ED

First published 1993

Reprinted 1994

Reprinted 1995

Reprinted 1996

ISBN 0 901762 93 8

Printed in Great Britain by
St Edmundsbury Press Ltd., Bury St Edmunds, Suffolk

Contents

Introduction

This is not another National Curriculum book

It's about something more important than the National Curriculum, and could be the key to making the whole National Curriculum work. It's a book about feeling good, about self-esteem: yours, the children's of course, and that of everyone in and around the school.

It's about primary classroom practice. It's about people - all the people that make up a school, and how we can make these people feel good about what they are doing.

This is important because self-esteem is important to children, teachers and everybody connected with the school community. It is at the heart of all our learning.

People learn best when they feel able to cope with their learning; feeling positive is the best condition for learning to take place, and good self-esteem is at the heart of feeling positive. It makes classroom life and relationships easier, makes for a happier atmosphere, makes what we all learn more productive and rewarding and is more likely to make us get up and do more.

This book may not be about the National Curriculum but it does respond in a positive, practical way to current concerns and pressures. It is a book which tackles the growing feeling that teachers somehow need to prove their worth. It is a timely book, though self-esteem is not of momentary importance: it is always current, timeless as well as timely, because, whatever the pressures, whatever the situation, it is always at the heart of what happens.

A school which tries to become a community actively promoting self-esteem, will find itself becoming a place where people want to be and want to work, where people feel confident about learning. But the task is more than that of raising the self-esteem of the children, making them feel good about themselves. It is concerned with the growth of everyone's self-esteem, every child, every member of the staff, every member of the school community.

FEELING GOOD ABOUT YOURSELF

SO HOW DO I START?

With yourself. The first thing to do is to recognise how much you are doing for everyone else and their self-esteem and how important that is. You may not think of what you are doing as raising self-esteem, you probably call it doing your job. Stop and look at what you do each day. You may be called a teacher, but how many rôles does that involve? In one day you may have been called on to be a nurse, friend, arbitrator, parent, guide, artist, salesperson, actor, manager, playmate, cashier, cook.................., or several of these at the same time.

An activity you might like to try for yourself is to make a list (or some drawings) of all the hats you have worn today.

Did you include...health promoter, judge, police officer, counsellor, scientist.......?

'Hats' I have worn today.

Look through your list again. When did you wear these hats? Did you choose to do so, or were you forced into it? Did you find yourself wearing more than one at the same time? How many times while accepting these rôles did you also find yourself boosting someone's self-esteem?

For instance;

When you were a nurse did you make

Peggy ~
- doing three things at the same time
- listening & speaking at the same time
- speed, organisation
- expert - in everything! coffee maker, detective, finding people and things
- carrying out orders, confidence in my own judgement
- listening ear, patience, tolerance, keeping confidences.
- buffer between people and sets of people
- supplies officer.
- time keeper, record keeper, keyboard skills, repair skills, first aid technological skills.
- not going to the loo until its desperate!

more than that grazed knee better?

When you were a friend did the person recognise you as a true friend and feel even better?

When you were an arbitrator did those involved see another's point of view and feel better?

Try doing this activity with a colleague or with the whole staff - teaching and non-teaching. The staff of one school used this activity at the start of an inset day looking at ways of improving the relationships in the school and the quality of motivation for everyone concerned.

On these pages are two of their lists, one compiled by a teacher, one by the part-time school secretary.

Jan –

- time management, person management
  child management
- observer, researcher, reporter
  decision maker.
- translation of written + spoken word.
- friend, ally
- skilled in making others skilled.
- tea/coffee maker, time + record keeper.
- patience, saying the same thing
  in a different way
- listener, speaker, reader, writer
- doing several things at same time.
- preventer of problems, chaos avoider,
  problem solver.
- dramatic skills, artistic + presentation
  skills
- finder of lost anything
- nurse policeman parent.

Notice the way in which both of them grouped their skills.

The group was slow to get started, at first perhaps unaware of the extent of their skills. They were encouraged to move from a silent individual approach into small groups, sharing ideas. One of the most frequently overheard statements was:

"Well - if you put it that way, then that's what I do."

Once they got started there was no stopping them. It certainly boosted their self-esteem. Try it - it could boost yours.

Now try a quick check of all the skills have you been called on to use in school today? How many more can you add?

Now try a quick check of skills you have been called on to use in school today?

Organisation	Presentation	Negotiation
Display	Observation	Delegation
Listening	Story-telling	Rehearsal
Team-management	Forward-planning	
....	....	....

What about the feelings you have experienced or shared in school today?

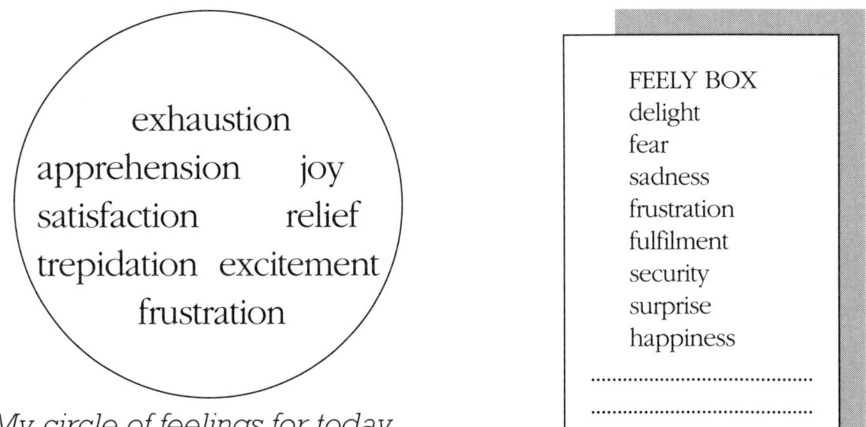

exhaustion
apprehension
joy
satisfaction
relief
trepidation
excitement
frustration
FEELY BOX
delight
fear
sadness
frustration
fulfilment
security
surprise
happiness
....
....

My circle of feelings for today

Did you share any of these feelings with anyone?

Was it someone in school or outside school?

Did it help to talk about your feelings?

Did you share any of your feelings with the children?

Did that help? How?

How many of these feelings have you helped children to express, even if you haven't used those words? Did it help them? How?

Here are some ideas we have tried:

Joseph's great grandpa died on Sunday.
Joseph was very sad.
Nobody talked about it at home nor when he was there.
He wanted to talk, so he told us. We were all sad.

Mrs Patel read us the story called Badgers Parting Gifts It was sad but good at the end. Some of us cried.

Mandy and me we helped Joseph make a book about his great grandfather and all the things he had shown people how to do. Joseph said that his great grandfather told the best stories ever.
Joseph cried then.

Lee Ann is new in our class.
She only came on Monday.
She was upset.
She kept getting lost.
She did'nt think anyone liked her.
Some one said something unkind.
We felt terrible

~ SO ~

we talked about being new and how it feels.
Lee Ann told us.
We collected "feeling new" words.
Lee Ann had lots.
We are helping her settle in and choose new friends.
We all felt better.

"Feeling New" words.

nobody likes me.

all alone

outside the circle

want to go back home

late

lost

different

last

shy

want to cry

want to hide

when did you feel like this?

Mrs Bottley found a story called Moving House. It was funny and sad at the same time.

Patrick

Amy and me found a long thin poem about being new. It was in Feelings by Aliki. We read it with Lee Ann. She said it was good.

WHAT ABOUT MY OWN SELF-ESTEEM?

The way you feel about yourself must have an effect upon the way you feel about the people around you and the way they feel about you. This is particularly so in the classroom. Feeling good can be contagious. A key feature of feeling good about yourself is knowing that you and your feelings are valued and accepted. What better way to boost self-esteem, the children's and your own? Encourage the children to know this, to boost the self-esteem of others. Let them boost yours and recognise that they are doing this. Too often in our school and classroom life, pressured as it often is, we fail to recognise the self-esteem boosters, or dismiss them as everyday routines.

Stop and look back over the past few days. When did someone do something which made you feel good, or made you feel better? You don't have to make written lists, but it's a good idea. It helps you to see how much you and others do, and how skilled you are at doing it.

MY SELF-ESTEEM WAS BOOSTED WHEN........

BOOSTER BOX

Did someone.
Make your tea?
Ask you for help or advice?
Who was it?
Why did they ask you?
Offer you some help?
Why did they offer?
Make you feel valued?
Was it something they said or did?
How did you respond?

Have any of the children boosted your self-esteem recently? When? Where? Was it something a child or some children said or did? How did you respond?

You could try this activity just before you go to sleep at night. It's better than counting sheep, or brooding on attainment targets.

Taken separately, these may seem to be small insignificant happenings, but gathered together, built up day by day, they will reinforce your self-esteem, make you feel good - or better - about what you are doing and achieving. You could try the same activity with the children, encouraging and enabling them to reflect on their days, on what they have done in and out of school. You will be teaching them the positive skills of recognising and celebrating the many small happenings which have made them feel good about themselves. It may seem an unusual activity to them at first, but with practice they will become quite adept. The children may be happy simply to talk about the feeling good happenings, but they will enjoy and benefit from making some kind of ongoing record which they can refer to and extend. Work with the children to invent their own pictorial ways of doing this recording. Suggest your own ways: invite other colleagues and other classes to share their ideas. (One school had so many ideas that they made a staff reference notebook, much valued by all, but especially by teachers newly appointed to the school.)

Try building up a 'Feeling good about myself ' wall.

Try building up a flower, petal by petal: a plant, leaf by leaf; apples on a tree; washing hanging up on a line; a train, truck by truck. Try using the computer to devise a technique using a paint or draw program.

Invite the children to invent a colour coding system to distinguish between feeling good happenings in the school, in the classroom, on the way to and from school, at home, in the community, things people said and things people did.

Feeling Good

Here are some of the things which have made us feel good about ourselves. You can work out who made us feel good, what they said and did and where it happened.

Mrs. Green says I was today's best helper

I went upstairs in the dark by myself

JENNY

Grandpa came to tea and said I was a great footballer

Mr. Larkins said you're a sensible girl, you are

Sandy says I'm his girlfriend

(yellow – at home)
(red – in school)
(green – outside)

Ella said tie my shoes you're good at knots

Daniel asked me to his house to tea

Dad said I'm a good car washer

Manjit helped me with my work

The paint spilled, lots of people mopped me up

Tammy shared her crisps with me

Mum liked the way I looked after our baby

Mrs Patel said I worked REALLY hard today

ALEX

(red – things people said
green – things people did)

I Said I was sorry to Benji and it was my fault

My mummy, she said I make the best cuppa in the house

My gran gave me a hug when nobody could see

jumped in the swimming pool, I was scared but I did it.

My dog cuddled up to me to watch T.V.

lex and Hassit said come and with us today.

Wen Carrie bullied me, Jody said don't, he's my friend

blue – family
green – friends
black – my dog
red – grown-ups
purple – ME

Have you helped some one feel good today?

What did you do?
what did you say?
what did the person say?

Here are some other ideas the children might like to try.

Invite the children to include at least one positive thing they have done or said which has made them feel good or better about themselves.

You may have to spell it out to the children at first, to make them stop and think and try to put into words how feeling good about themselves actually feels. Ask them to recall one happening, one occasion when someone said or did something to make them feel good. How did they feel, inside themselves? You might try starting them off with a few obviously inappropriate words and phrases, such as "Didn't you feel cold? Shaky? Shivery? Scared stiff? Well- if you didn't feel any of these things, how *did* you feel?"

You could collect up the children's responses in a circle of feeling good words.

It is then only a small step towards looking at ways of making other people feel good or better. Children can look at things they can do, say, not say, ways of supporting friends, helping others in difficult situations, particularly where bullying, name-calling or coercion is evident. This activity, while not specifically devised to tackle abuse of this kind, often results in these issues being raised by the children themselves. You can develop the discussion to look at ways of helping children who are being bullied to feel better about themselves, and to find the necessary strategies and strength to cope.

It may then be possible to look at people who bully, to ask if they do in fact feel good about themselves. The children may then be able to think of strategies to help the bully reflect on what is being inflicted.

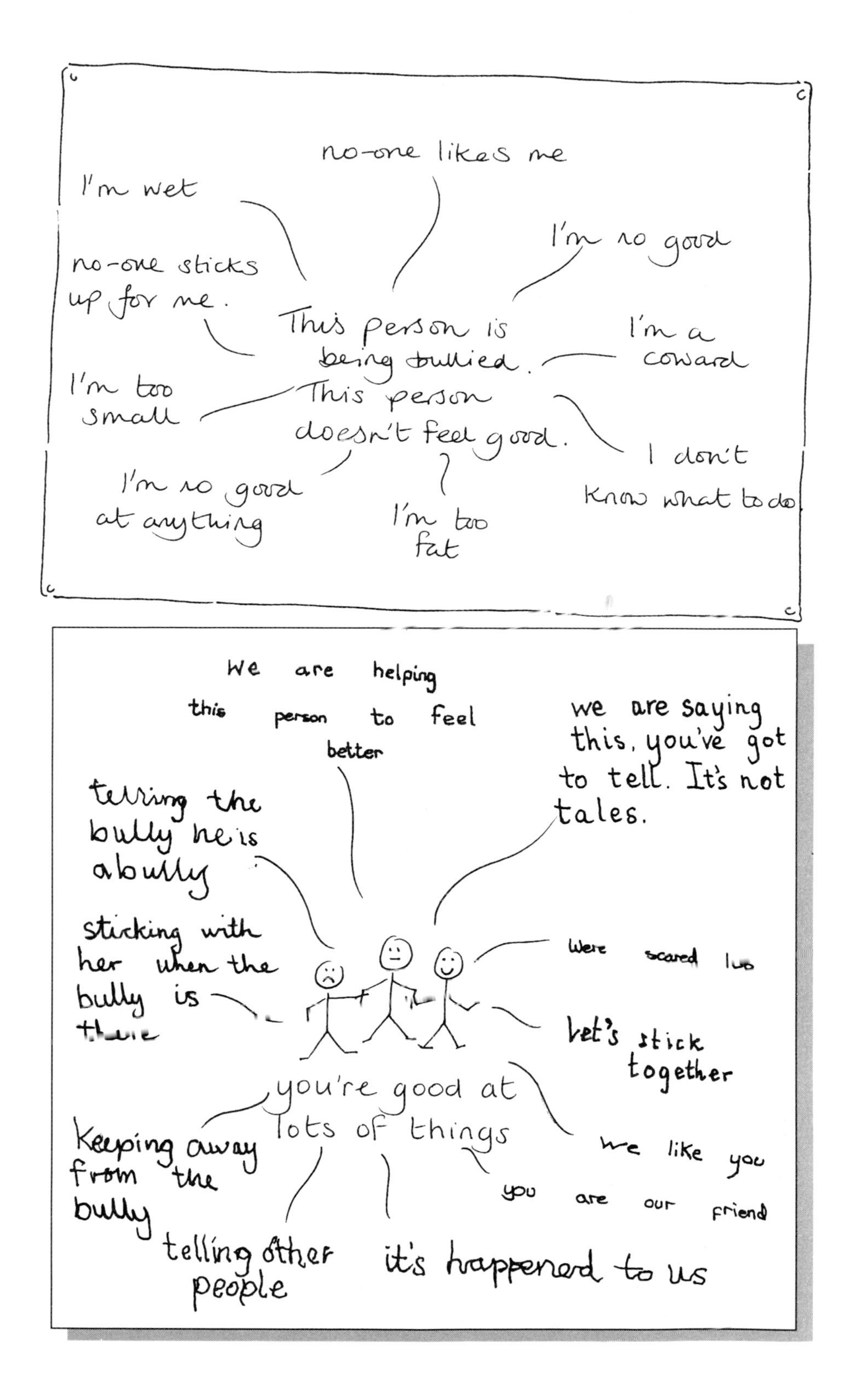
no-one likes me
I'm wet
I'm no good
no-one sticks up for me.
This person is being bullied.
I'm a coward
I'm too small
This person doesn't feel good.
I don't know what to do
I'm no good at anything
I'm too fat
We are helping this person to feel better
we are saying this, you've got to tell. It's not tales.
telling the bully he is a bully
sticking with her when the bully is
Were scared
let's stick together
you're good at lots of things
Keeping away from the bully
we like you
you are our friend
telling other people
it's happened to us

But when did you boost your own self-esteem? When did you stop and recall all the small or great achievements of your day? Or hold them up, count them, and say "Well done you!" ?

When did you last say:

"That went well!"

"The kids have done a smashing display in our room"

"I used to find that difficult, but now......"

"Hey, that was a great lesson!"

"What a lot I've got through today!"

"I'd never have believed I could do that!"

Or................do you usually remember the things that went wrong?

From now on, for a change, try making a list of Everything That Went Right Today. What about things which you had never done before, or things which just went better than before?

Everything That Went O.K. Today

Try using these headings:

What have I tried today that I've never tried before?

What have I done today better than before?

Who are the people I have helped today?

Who has helped me today?

What gave me the most pleasure today?

Could these lists include delight, laughter, surprise, success, sharing disaster ....?

It is a small step from making lists to taking time out to reflect, review and praise yourself. You could surprise yourself by how much you've done, how much of yourself you've given, what you've achieved.

Who has helped me today?

Alice
George
Dilwar
Mrs Cox
Gordon

Remember, for the people around you to feel good, you need to feel good about yourself. The starting point is you.

Three Things I Did Well Today

There are many ways of helping yourself to feel good. Build up a network of people around you, in and out of school to share what you are doing and trying to do. Include your hopes, achievements, concerns, disappointments, and disasters. Share this with the children, share it, if you can, with the children's families, share it with every member of the school community. And when there is no one around to share it with, share it with yourself, in your head. Or try writing it down and reading it through. Let this become a regular feature of your day.

Expect good things to happen and they will
Be yourself.
Be a performer.
Be a brilliant performer sometimes - but not a pretender.
Be honest with the children, and yourself.
Be open about your feelings, your needs, how much you care, do, want to do, when you need space and quiet, when you need help.

You could use the list-making activity as part of your In-service programme. It makes a positive start to an after-school session, when people are exhausted.

This list came from a whole school staff, including all the non-teaching staff, who were asked to think of things that had gone well during the day, or brilliantly if they thought this word was appropriate.

After a few moments of uncertainty, modesty was overcome and their lists began to grow. At the end of two or three minutes they were asked to stop and share their contributions in small groups. Finally, they were persuaded to display the shared contribution for everyone to see.

Things we excelled at today

Keeping calm

getting through most of what I'd planned

settling arguments

motivating the children

assembly — though the children did most of it

listening to three children at once

reading a story — it had them sitting on the edges of their chairs

turning a difficult situation around so that it became positive

circle time with reception, we used it all day

getting children to listen to each other for a few moments

organising P.E. so that we got going on time.

You could take this activity a step further by asking yourself (or a group of colleagues) to look at all you do each day to support, help, and boost children and others you work with. Reflect on that for a few minutes. Add it to the lists you have made about yourself, your skills, talents and achievements. That should boost you and your self-esteem.

Stop for a moment and ask yourself why you do all this, every day, despite the increasing pressures on you and your time and energy. It isn't written down in your contract. No one except you evaluates and assesses it. Yet you go on doing it. Why?

It's because you know it works, because you know it can change classroom life, relationships and attitudes. What's more, it's like any other skill, activity or sport: the more you practise, the better you get at it, and the more it works.

It is a concern for all teachers to present themselves in a positive light for appraisal by their peers and others, but this process can become a negative and demeaning activity if approached with low self-esteem. So, feel good about yourself, take time out to reflect, review and praise yourself. Use the activities we have described to remind yourself of all the positive aspects of your teaching. This will help you feel more confident about your own performance, and, in the rôle of appraiser, will help you to share the positive attributes of your colleagues.

WHAT HAVE WE SAID SO FAR?
That this is a book about classroom life, not the National Curriculum. It's about self-esteem. The self-esteem of everyone involved in that classroom life.
It's about starting with yourself, establishing your own self-esteem, discovering how much you do each day, how much you contribute to making others feel good.
It's about finding a few minutes each day to reflect on the processes of that day, on all that has been achieved and feeling good about it.
And it's about enabling others to use this reflective process, particularly the children.

Helping Other People to Feel Good

Once you have given your own self-esteem a chance to grow, you become more aware of other people, esteeming them, learning how important their self-esteem is to them.

The next step is to look at what you are already doing in your classroom which boosts the self-esteem of the children. How can you build on that?

We all know that the ethos of the classroom - any classroom, every classroom - needs to be positive with everyone's contribution being valued. There needs to be an atmosphere of happiness, security, fulfilment, and delight. Within this atmosphere children should feel they have permission to be afraid, to fail, to be sad, to be angry - sometimes.

We know it's not easy to do this, along with everything else required of us, but expect good things of each child, of the class, of the day, of yourself, and they will happen. Work with children at their eye level. Give yourself permission to work alongside children, play alongside, to read, write, paint, rest alongside (if there's ever time to rest!). This is a wonderful opportunity to listen in to what the children say, to the words they use and how they use them, words they know and need to know. You will see ways to help them and you can discover how much they know. But don't be afraid to stand back when you need to, help the children to understand that sometimes we all need space to grow and to be ourselves.

A Positive Language for the Classroom

Recognise that the language we use, and the responses we make, reflect the way we value those we are with and the contributions they make, that the words we use in our everyday classroom transactions can easily create positive or negative images and feelings.

We have become increasingly aware of gender and race in terms of classroom language, but the common currency of the classroom can often unintentionally belittle children and their contributions.

Consider the implications to the children of referring to *scrap paper*, or talking about *rough work, rough books, doing it in rough first.*

What value are we placing on children's preliminary efforts when we describe them in this way?

Instead, try referring to any kind of material, used for drafting, by other names, such as: Ideas books
Working books
Thinking books
Drafting books
Ideas sheets
Thinking paper
Draft copy paper

Try saying: "*Let's talk with..........*" rather than "*Let's talk to...........*"

for example, "*Let's talk with your parents to see if they can help us with the visit*" or "*Let's talk with the people in the Information Centre. They might be able to suggest the most interesting place to go.*"

Encourage the children to talk about borrowing and sharing each other's ideas rather than to see this as copying or cheating.

Copying can imply a lack of ownership and originality, and fails to reflect the effort the children have put into the work, whereas borrowing acknowledges the shared source of the words but also implies ownership of the ideas and room for originality. Consider the implications of these words *copying, copied, copy* as the children, and even we ourselves, use them. We only need to listen to children, as they work alongside each other, to know that when someone says "Miss, he's copying from me" the child thinks that her or his ideas are being stolen. Can we not encourage children to think in terms of sharing and borrowing each other's ideas, to feel good about being the sharer and the borrower. If we use these words ourselves in talking about the day's activities then the children will begin to use the same language.

Try saying "*Share your ideas with the person next to you, or with your group*" instead of saying "*Talk about it*" or "*Discuss it*".

Try collecting the children's ideas and vocabulary on the chalkboard or flipchart under the heading

Ideas to borrow

We are just starting our topic on

Words you might like to borrow.

You could thank the children who offer these ideas and check that it is OK for others to borrow them. When the time comes to write, remind the children that they are choosing the words they want to use. If a child is unable to locate a word or phrase to borrow, you or someone else could help. Gradually the notion of borrowing words will grow. You could remind children, when they are writing, that words they need can be found in many places - in their own heads (the best place) - collected on the chalkboard - around the classroom - in books of all kinds - in other people's heads.

Remind the children to use the words borrow and borrowed when they show their work to their friends and to parents and families. When someone praises a piece of their work and asks

"*Did you copy it?*" remind the children to say

"*No, of course not! I borrowed some of the words I needed, but I wrote it. I did it myself.*"

MINDING THE SHOP

You could reinforce this idea of borrowing and sharing by introducing a walkabout activity sometimes. You can use it when the whole class is working in pairs or small groups, perhaps, on one aspect of a topic. You can also use it when groups are working on quite different activities. You will need to introduce the walkabout idea gradually, asking the children to tell you what can be gained from sharing and borrowing each other's ideas like this. Start by asking them to negotiate or nominate one person in the group to be the 'shopkeeper', the one who, when the rest of the group circulates, will stay behind at the group table or area, and explain to any 'customers' what is being done, what is being achieved, and what problems have been met. Then, at a given moment, perhaps the end of the session, invite the class to go and look round the other groups, to ask questions, to offer advice. If time permits, ask the group to change the shopkeepers, so that they have an opportunity to circulate too. Remind the children as they return to their groups that borrowing and sharing ideas is a positive thing, something which makes classroom life better. It is useful to the borrowers, and makes the lenders feel good. You could ask sometimes

" *Who shared an idea with someone else?*"

" *Who borrowed an idea from someone else? Did you say "thanks - that was a good idea*"?

One class of nine and ten year olds decided that it would be helpful if they clarified the rules of the Minding the Shop activity. They worked in groups first before making a set of class instructions and rules.

A class of children in year two used the technique in a topic relating to museums. Each group set up a mini-museum reflecting aspects of the topic work. Minding the Shop became a regular feature of their working. They demonstrated and explained the technique to other classes and to visitors on an open day.

As an introduction to this activity with younger children, you can

Instructions for minding the shop.

Time Topic Work.
Organisation, in groups.

This is what you do:
1. Stop working and talk about how you are getting on, your good ideas, problems and ways round.
2. Make sure everyone can explain what your group is doing and why you are doing it that way and what you plan to do next.
3. Choose a shop keeper to mind the shop and explain to other people.
4. Everyone else go round QUIETLY to see how other groups are getting on BORROW and share GOOD IDEAS PROBLEMS and SOLUTIONS

Don't forget, to give your shopkeeper a go

say thanks to people

Philip Lee.
Mary Ellis
Kevin Burlson

invite them to work in pairs, sharing their ideas and putting them on paper as pictures, or as words and pictures. You can then ask the children in their pairs to number themselves 1 and 2. Invite all the number 1's to leave their pictures behind and go round looking at - borrowing, sharing and praising - other people's ideas. When they return, their partners are then free to go. They can then share with each other, with you or with all the class what they have achieved, and how sharing and borrowing has helped them. Don't forget to join in yourself and tell the children what you gained.

This approach to the sharing and borrowing of ideas makes the introduction of acknowledging quotations from reference books much easier for writers to come to terms with. How many of

Healthy People

Today we all had to draw pictures of healthy people.

We shared our pictures with our partners.

Then we went walking around the room to look at other people's pictures.

We borrowed and we shared lots of good ideas.

notion that the students had adopted and applied the health enhancing strategy. They seemed to have adopted this strategy by means of addressing issues which were close to them, i.e. mainly psychological and social health issues. Yet, when the strategy had been adopted, the students proceeded to carry out health-enhancing activities relating to physical health as well as to psychological and social health.

It was possible to discern four different types of processes (*groups I–IV*). Some students were very active, while other participated reluctantly. The outcomes, however, in these four groups did not differ significantly. This finding might partly be due to small numbers. Yet, it nevertheless indicates that the way of adopting a health-enhancing strategy differs vastly between different individuals. Moreover, the observations done by the health counsellors did not predict the outcome for the individual students. Thus, it seemed justified to rely on the student's own way of using the method, even in situations when the health counsellor felt dubious about progress of the student.

Since the control students, as well as the experimental students, had volunteered to enroll for the programme, this group also got the opportunity to participate, albeit after the post-test. Therefore it was not possible to study long term effects in this material.

Thus, the results indicate that behavioural effects, relating to physical health, may indeed be achieved by a student-centred school health education model. In addition, the intervention resulted in an increase of health-enhancing activities concerning psychological and social health.

Programme dissemination

In the method studied students were *invited* to participate. They were not expected to enroll due to their mere presence in the compulsory school. An analogous attitude was adopted at other levels; in the recruitment of health counsellors and in the recruitment of headmaster districts. Moreover, in 'It's your decision' the starting point was the student, not the subject. In an analogous way, by the dissementation of the method, the starting point has been the needs of the students, as perceived by the school staff. The health counsellors, after the recommended two-days introduction course, have been encouraged to transform the method to the local needs. All particularities of the method but two, have

been left open to question. The only principles we thought were not negotiable were the non-judgemental approach to the students, and the health counsellors' readiness to listen to them.

Out of this it follows that a central control of the dissemination of the method in the target area was neither possible nor desirable. The attitude of the project team was to offer a *tool* to the schools. This is analogous to the task of the health counsellor i.e. to offer to the student a *tool* for their health-enhancement. This attitude might well be too liberal in other circumstances. In the school system, however, where compulsion is the rule, we thought such an attitude was necessary, if the adolescent students were to make use of the intervention.

A major spin-off effect has been training of school staff. The health counsellors were recruited on the basis of their interest in a student-centred method. Therefore you might expect that these persons were already used to approaching the students with an open mind. Yet, in the evaluations of the training-courses for health counsellors, including the supervision sessions, these persons often have said that their skill in listening to the students had been much improved.

Address

Sven Bremberg
Subdivision of School Health,
Department of Pediatrics and
Department of Community Medicine
Faculty of Health Sciences,
University of Linköping,
Sweden.

References

1. *Green, L. W.* Some challenges to health service research on children and the elderly. Health Serv. Research 1985; 19: 793–815.
2. *Bartlett, E. E.* The contribution of school health education to community health promotion: what can we reasonably expect? Am. J. Publ. Health 1981; 71: 1384–1391.
3. *Green, L. W.* Health education models. In: Matarazzo, J. D. *et al.* (Eds). Behavioral Health. New York: John Wiley & Sons, 1984.
4. *Connell, D. B., Turner, R. R. and Mason, E. F.* Summary of findings of the school health education evaluation: health promotion effectivness, implementation, and costs. J. Sch. Health 1985; 55: 316–321.
5. *Loring, K. and Laurin, J.* Some notions about assumptions underlying health education. Health Educ. Q. 1985; 12: 231–243.
6. *American Public Health Association.* Criteria for the development of health promotion and education programs.

us struggled with our consciences when we first wrote an academic essay which included just these sorts of borrowed ideas? How many primary school children understand that this is an accepted practice for many adults?

Displays of Sharing

You could help them to understand this by the way you display their work in and out of the classroom. At the same time you will be helping them to feel good about their individual contributions. Remind them that one of the purposes of displaying their finished work is to share it with others and to show what they have achieved, as a class.

Talk with the children about strategies they could use to persuade people to stop, look, enjoy and learn from the work displayed, and to recognise the amount of effort involved. You could then suggest a quotation strategy. The children and you would read through the work displayed and select statements, descriptions, summaries which would make interesting quotations and which would draw in the passers-by and encourage them to read more. These quotations could then be written in larger, bolder, coloured and different print and could surround the display, or you could make use of simple paper engineering techniques to make pop-ups, flap-outs and pull-downs, to involve them actively in acknowledging the source or inviting viewers to find it.

Who said "we didn't know when we began, what we had let ourselves in for".

'Someone said "writing down what you are observing is very difficult" who was it? Did anyone else have this problem?

Lewis used some unusual words to describe the experiment his group did. Can you find them? Did you know these words?

Abbie's summary took 6 lines. Can you find a shorter one?, a longer one? Do they all say the same thing?

Girling wrote about "something effervescing over the top" what did she mean? what made it effervesce?

Class or group books provide similar opportunities:

We are always aware that it is important when displaying or presenting work to include a contribution from each child. You can reinforce the importance of each child's contribution by adding to the work displayed a list of all the people involved, whatever their rôle. The children themselves can be part of doing this. They will suggest their own ways of classifying or categorising the list of contributors.

In this book you will find 7 stories:

3 stories about real people in real places

2 stories about pretend people in real places

1 story about tropical birds

1 story about pretend people in pretend places.

See if you can find the authors of these quotations:

Nonsuch opened the gate and there stood the Great Green Gloop.

— darting swooping swifting swirling never resting

No, No Snip, No, No Snap Don't go into the kitchen

What a terrible day said Henry to himself. What will tomorrow be?

They never found it again but they keep looking.

Who worked on this picture of Autumn?

Amy
Andrew
Kirsty
Liam
Sharina
Asif

Mrs Baker and
Mrs Khaldi
did the sticking
and climbing up
the wall.

Who worked on this topic display?

We did – Marylou and Natasha we like working together.

Nikki Wood from the library
Wayne Babey from the museum
Our teacher Mrs Zanetti
Lots of Mums
Lots of Dads

• The Topic Expert Company:

• Leslie
• Fahoum
• Grace
• Bennie
• Adam
• Manjit
• Rophina

Encourage them to think back through all the stages of the work and to collect up, by name, all the contributors. This could include older children in the class, people within the school, from the family and the community and could include:

providers of ideas and materials
solvers of problems
authors, illustrators, researchers and proof-readers
those who prepared and mounted the display and graphics
those responsible for the continued care of the display

You probably won't need to remind them gently that you too had a rôle to play.

Children (and adults) enjoy showing others their contributions to displays of work. They each want to be able to say

"*Look, that's a bit I did*"
"*That's my writing*"
"*I helped with that picture*"
"*Our group did that*"

You reinforce this even further if you make a Visitors Book so that other people can record that they have seen and appreciated the children's work. The children will want to take on board the responsibility for showing visitors what they have done, explaining all that went into it, and inviting signatures and comments.

We can celebrate the children's contributions, make them more rewarding, by the way we use their names, by setting out, as boldly as we can, the rôle each has played. We can help them and others to recognise the quality of the process of making a shared presentation as well as to enjoy the finished object.

USING NAMES

Use names a lot, help children to realise that people's names are very special to them and to value each other's names, not to alter them without permission.

Whenever possible refer to people by name, not by occupation - Mrs. Porter who helps to keep our school clean.

"*Go and ask Mrs. Porter*" not "*Go and ask the caretaker*"

"*Mr. O'Gorbly who is in charge of the school-crossing patrol*" - not "*the lollipop man*"

"*This is Mrs. Jones, our new helper at dinner time*" -

Not "*The new dinner lady*"

not "*That Miss*"

Reinforce this idea by using people's names as well as titles on doors and notices

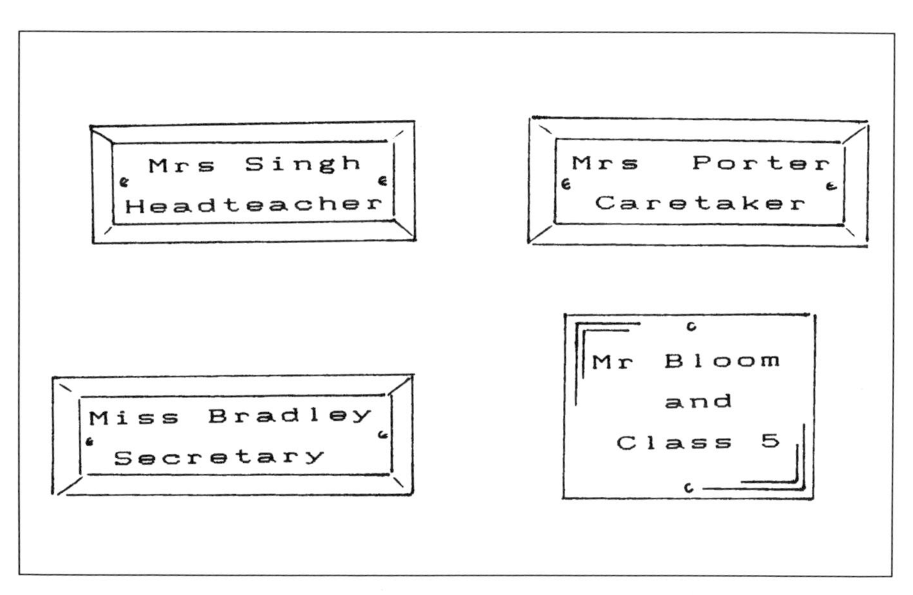

Talk about the names children prefer to be known by and those they don't like people using. Include yourself in this if it is appropriate.

My name is Jennifer Anna Clarke, somtimes my Gran calls me Jennyana.
Sometimes my big sister calls me Jen. I hate it!
My mum calls me Jennifer when she's cross and Jennifer Anna Clarke when she's very cross.
Mrs Patel asked me if I wanted her to call me Jennifer or Jenny I said "Jenny".
My very best friends call me Jack, can you guess why?

When a new child joins the class, ask, so that the class can hear

"What name do you like people to use when they talk with you?"

"This is Mary Lou. She likes to be called Mary Lou. Welcome to our class, Mary Lou."

or *"This is James McPherson. He likes to be called Jamie. Welcome to our class, Jamie."*

Look at names which can be given to, or used by, both girls and boys noting differences in spelling where this applies

Billie and Billy, Jack, Lee and Leigh, Sam, Alex, Charlie, George, Jo and Joe.

The children might be interested in looking at names where the girls and boys share the same root.

Henrietta	Henry	Georgina	George
Michelle	Michael	Alexandra	Alexander
Norma	Norman	Nichola	Nicholas

You could link this to some discussion of nicknames, diminutives of names, or talk about people with names chosen because of family traditions or to commemorate people, places, events, holy occasions.

You could build up a class photo board showing the children's preferred names. You could include your own picture and preferred name on this board.

Look at stories where the name plays an important part, such as *Call Me Harriet* or *The Turbulent Term of Tyke Tyler.*

Provide younger children with stand-up name cards and encourage them to use them as much as possible:

For display:

Make your own name card and use it

Encourage the children to make spares of their own design, decorated in different ways and to use them around the classroom. They

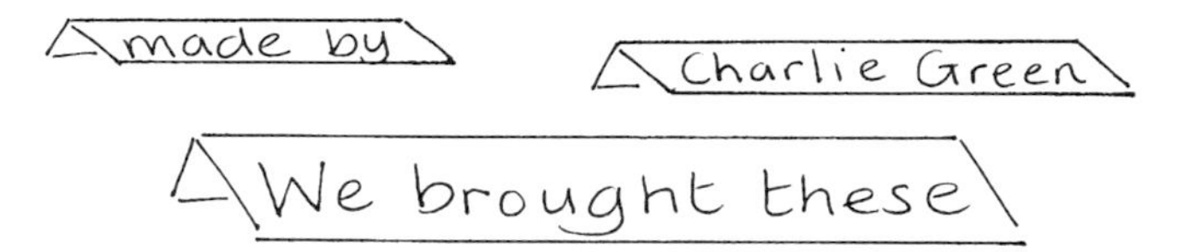

could use them to show ownership: particularly with younger children, when the putting up of a name card alongside something constructed or created is one way of making a personal statement.

To label work in progress

To display a shared activity, collection,or museum

To claim territory

The cards can be used to encourage some simple sentence making activities.

helped by   displayed by

Try adding some useful adaptable cards of your own.

Alexander   made this

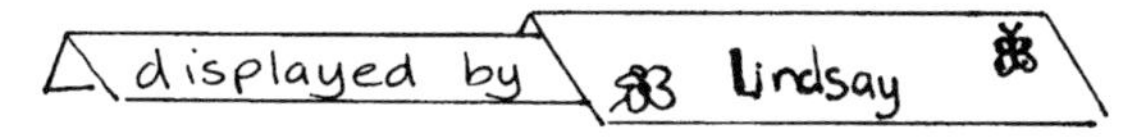

Children can then add their own name cards to construct statements which accompany their activities

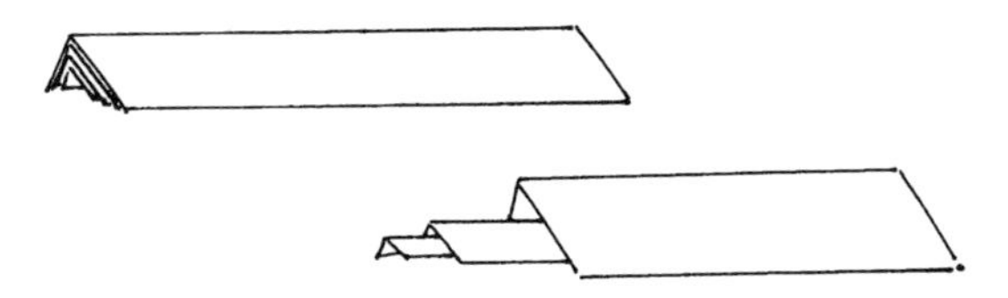

Children will begin to make their own stand-up cards, especially if

you leave a box of different size and shaped ready-folded paper.

An extension of these activities would be to have fun with their names, making amusing anagram name cards, acrostics and puzzles.

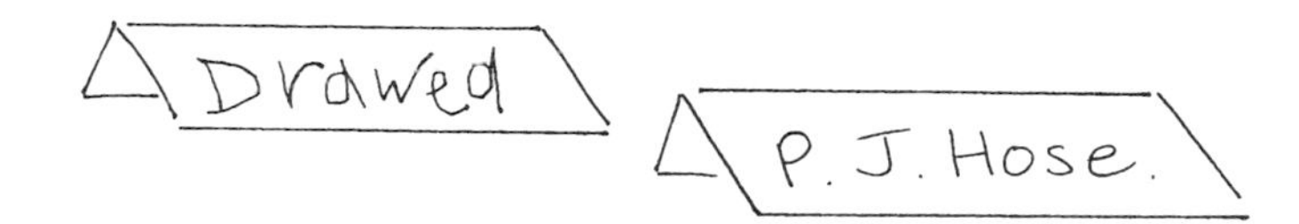

WHAT WAS THAT ALL ABOUT?
We started by looking at the language we use every day as currency in the classroom and the way it can shade the feelings we have about things. We suggested a number of small changes in the words we choose to use and implied that care should be taken over choosing the words used to encourage and praise, so that they really do that job.
We discussed the way in which the currency of ideas can be shared and borrowed in a positive manner, and suggested ways in which this could take place. We reinforced these suggestions with ideas for helping children to give and receive acknowledgement for contributions made to their work.
We looked at the use we make of people's names, respecting the names people prefer to be known by, suggesting ideas for looking at names positively, including the use of name cards for a variety of purposes, including early sentence construction.
We considered the way in which a more positive approach can help better self-esteem to generate more self-esteem. Many of the changes we have suggested in this section have been small but nonetheless significant. They can change the way a classroom works.

Using Circles

Circles themselves can be a very powerful means of communication. Think of the stone circles which attract so many people to them. (But we don't suggest you build Stonehenge in the classroom!) Instead try incorporating circles into your classroom life.

People Circles

There is a different atmosphere in the room, a sense of being equal, of being seen and being able to see everyone else when everyone sits in a circle, all at the same level, including the adults.

You can often learn how children relate to the rest of the group by watching as they form the circle. Some may decide to sit beyond the circle, demonstrating individuality or, perhaps loneliness. Some may feel that the circle is excluding them, be reluctant to push in and make a place for themselves. You could talk with the children about how they feel when they're getting into a circle, about what makes it difficult and how they could make it easier for each other.

The circle can be an ideal situation to discuss any issue. Ground rules for the class or school can be more easily established when all of those involved feel they can have an input. You could call this time Circle Time, Roundabout, Open Forum, Talkaround, The Staff Meeting, Sharing Time, Get Together. Even better, let the children invent their own names for the circle formation.

The class can be encouraged to start the day by sharing with each other some of the feelings they have had from the time they woke up to the time of arrival in the classroom. Most of us experience a wide range of feelings in this comparatively short space of time. Feelings may range from anticipation through frustration to relaxation. For some of us the feelings may be nothing more than routine concerns such as being at school on time, with all the right materials. For others, this hour or so

CIRCLE TIME

We meet once a day in circles
to talk and listen.
Sometimes one big circle,
sometimes group circles
We made some rules about it
We listen to people
We don't interrupt
We put our hands up if we want to speak
We try to understand people's feelings

Trevor Jane - Anna Elise

The infants have a kind of circle time
They call it News Time and they tell what
they have done
but
We talk about our
feelings

NEWS

Sometimes Mr Bernard
writes our feelings on
a big piece of paper.
We call it our circle
of feelings.
Sometimes we read it
again later in the day
and add new words.
Tuesday was a
worried day

TODAY'S CIRCLE OF
FEELINGS ABOUT THE TEST

bothered
trying to relax
worried
getting it right
new
prepared
not sure
hopeful

Tuesday March 9th

Ali & Lara

may be fraught with feelings difficult to cope with. Sharing in a circle, as a class or in a group, can be a way of understanding these feelings and learning how other people feel and behave.

Circle time can be equally valuable at the end of the morning or end of the day. The class can be encouraged to evaluate their days and reflect on the processes, interactions and qualities of classroom life, looking at what has made the day good for them and others.

A class of five and six year olds reflected on their day in terms of how they had felt. Their teacher acted as scribe as they built up their circle. The children were then asked to look for or draw some pictures to illustrate the feelings to supplement the teacher's quick sketches.

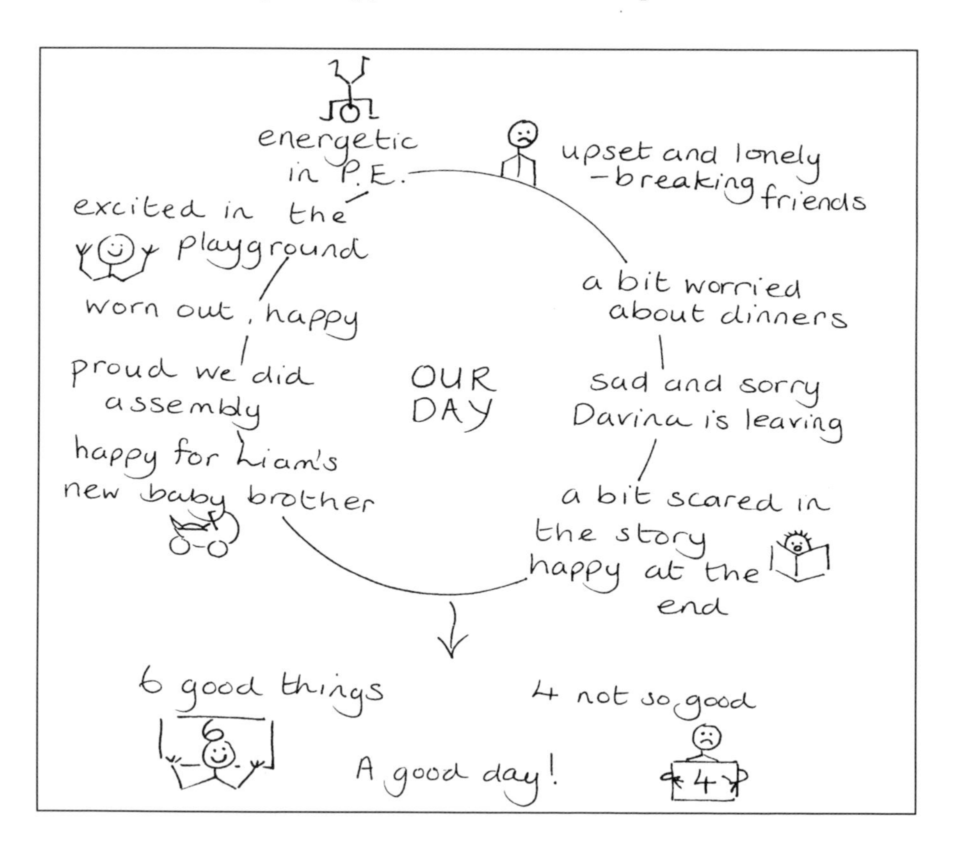

Don't forget to make your own contribution so that the children are reassured that you have the same kinds of feelings and that you are willing to put these into words.

Encourage the children to try to find the words and phrases to pin down exactly how they feel. Some of them may have a vocabulary of feelings limited to words such as mad, bad, glad, sad to describe the whole range of their emotions.

Circles of Feelings

Activities such as circles of feelings can encourage children to reflect on their feelings, put them into words and then share them with others in the class. They will need to feel confident about doing this and to discover that they can trust others.

They will need a growing language of feelings, one which takes them beyond the limitations of mad, bad, glad, sad.

Some children may not want or be able to share their feelings. Some may find them too strong to reflect on, to try to put into words, especially when these relate to fear, aggression, hatred, uncertainty, being bullied, anticipation, joy, love, delight.

It may be enough at the end of a circle time simply to thank the children for their contributions as both speakers, listeners and sharers of feelings. You could extend the activity by collecting some of the words and phrases which capture or sum up each child's feelings.

You could build these into a circle of feelings using a large sheet of paper or chalkboard, acting as scribe for the children and including each contributor's name, where you feel this is appropriate. When a new word or phrase is offered, you could ask the children to decide where it should be placed on the circle. Does the new word or phrase belong to others already written up or does it describe a new feeling, one not previously shared?

You could end the session by reading round the circle recalling the reasons for the feelings. You could make the circle grow by inviting the children to add pictures they have drawn or found. You could make a shared circle of feelings around many situations. For instance:

You could use it to talk about a wet playtime or Monday morning; as a way of responding to a visitor in school, a playground conflict, a visit to the dentist, bullying or being bullied, the death of a pet. You could use it as a way of helping the children to clarify their responses to a television or radio programme, to a video or to an educational visit.

You could use it to focus on a moment in a story or poem, exploring with the children how a character or group of characters might have

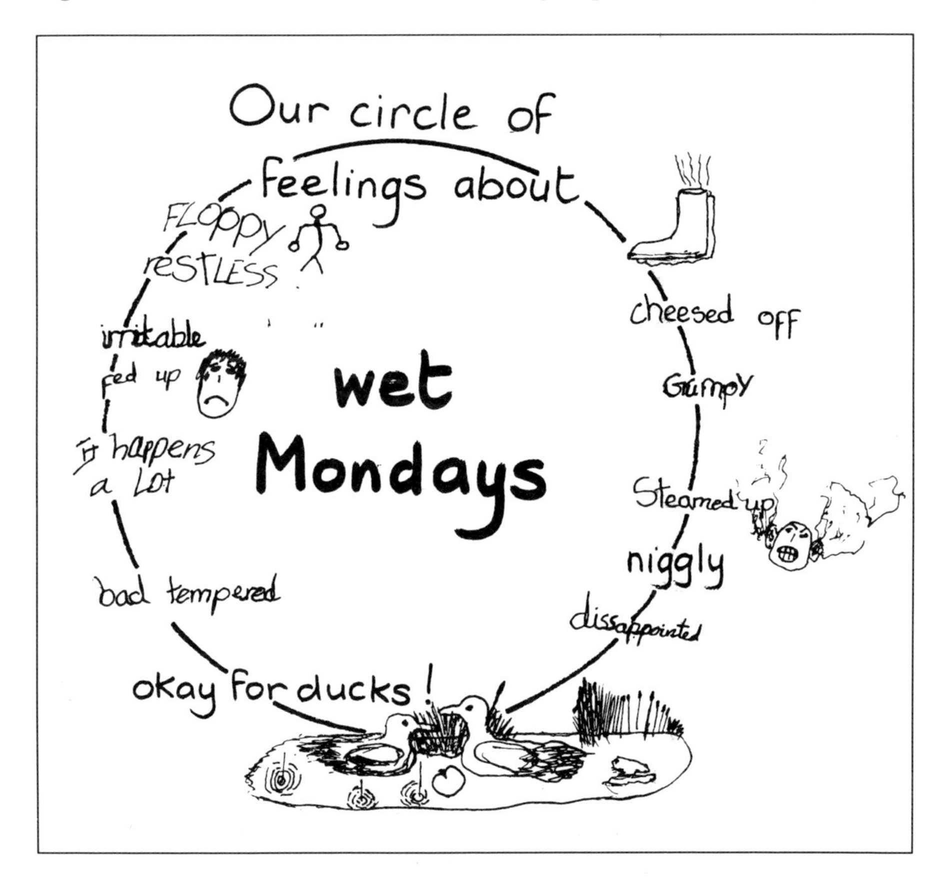

Can you draw paint or find some pictures to go with our circle of feelings?

Can you use these words to help you make even bigger sentences?

when ....
before ....
after ....
but ......
also ....

felt at that point. This could be a group activity, each group making its own circle of feelings.

Ask the children to decide where on the circle their words could go, helping them to cluster words with similar meanings and to discover opposites.

In the book about Lenny he felt......

Scared
SAD
crying
upset
By himself
WantED his Mum

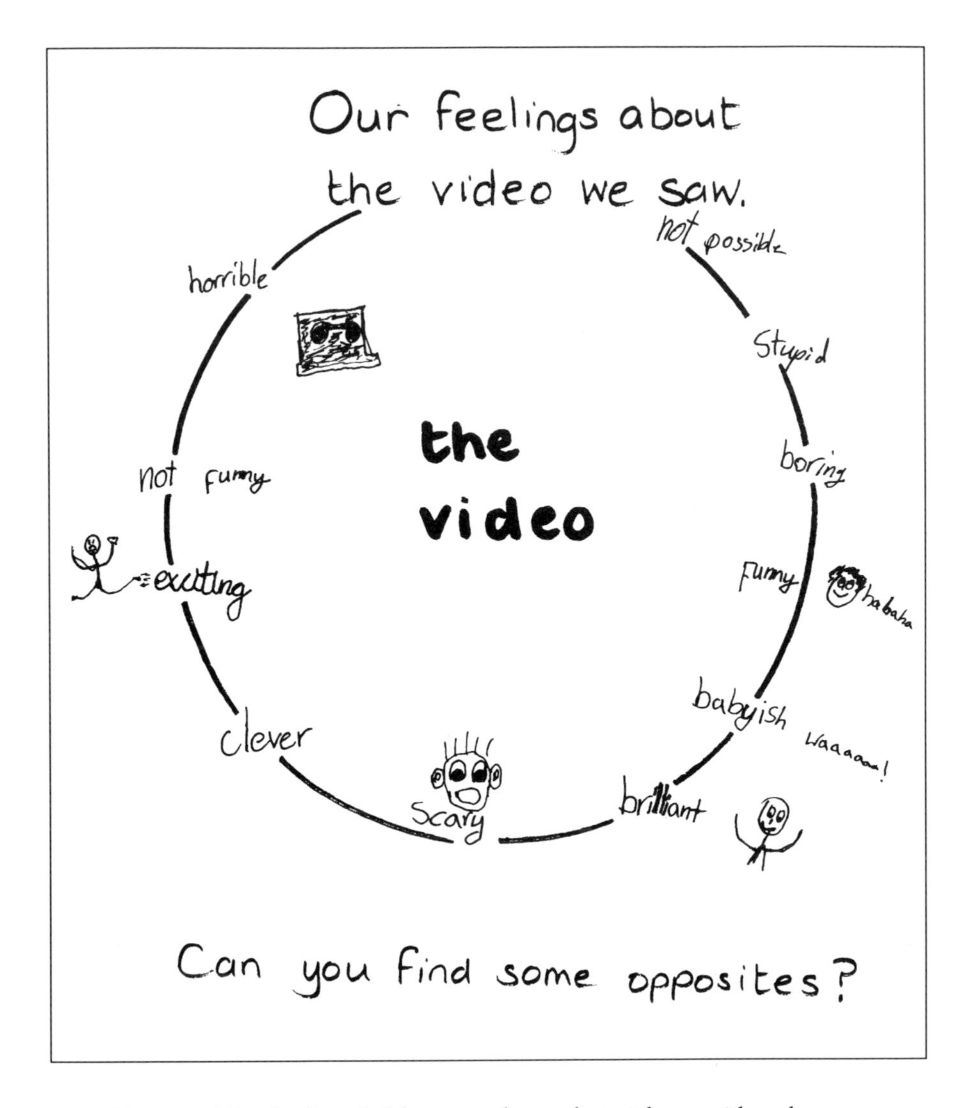

You could ask the children to share their ideas with other groups, to extend the language of their feelings. This would be a good opportunity to use the *Minding the Shop* strategy.

Encourage the children to value each other's contribution, by making positive comments.

We have made a circle of feelings about the story The Egg Man by Janni Howker.
We made it about the bit where Jane and Bridget went to see the Egg Man and he thought Jane was Nelly come back.

afraid to admit
scared and dared
risky
stupid
no sense
dangerus
not thinking what might happen
bravado
sensible
harmless
sympathetic
gentle
sorry for him
inquisitive
curious
nosy

Jane
Bridget
and the
Egg Man.

We shared our circle of feelings with the other groups doing a Minding The Shop
We got 44 different words and phrases altogether
We got lots of words and phrases meaning sensitive.
Mr. Sellars says there is a book called Sense and Sensitivity by Jane Austen written a long time ago.

You can then invite the children to display their work and to add to it. They might want to add new phrases or to illustrate the words they have collected. They could look for pictures from other sources, or draw and paint their own. They could extend the work further by looking for other areas of literature where a similar theme or situation is explored.

Word Circles

Try using circles when you are collecting the children's ideas on a chalkboard or flip chart and when you are presenting them with key words and phrases to use.

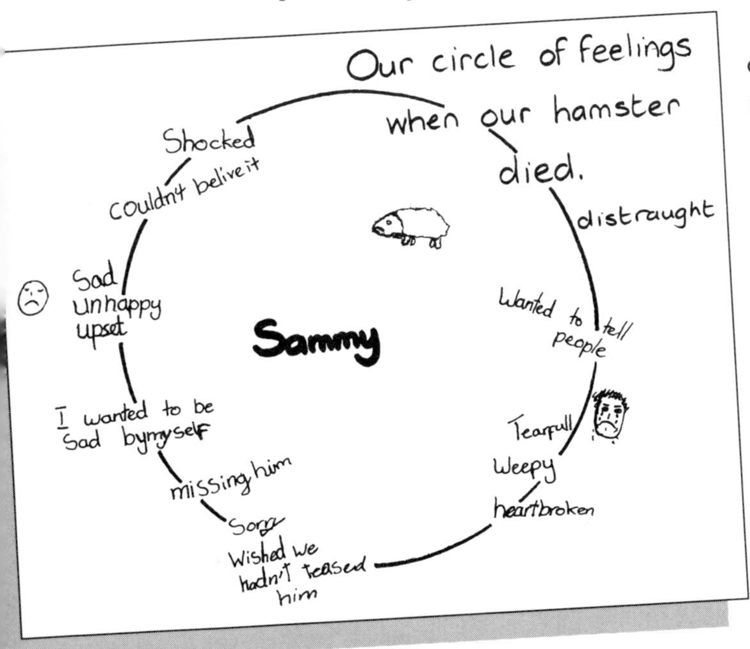

Word circles give every child's contribution equal value and status, and enable you and the children to cluster together words and phrases which extend the original ideas. In contrast listing words may suggest that one idea, word or phrase placed at the top, is better than others and should be used first. Some children may believe that ideas set out in a list must be used in that order, and not look further on for those which they need or want to use.

If words and phrases are scattered across the board without any discernible pattern, some children may be uncertain how to cope with the ideas and vocabulary on offer and therefore reluctant to start. When ideas are presented in a loose circle formation, the children can borrow the ideas and vocabulary for their own written work. They are more likely to look around the circle for the words they really want, to discover other, useful ones which have been put adjacent, and to use them in their own way. The resulting work will, through stemming from the shared starting point, be individual, personal and rewarding.

What we do to make us healthy
and keep us healthy.

enjoy being healthy
celebrate tell
messages

eat and drink
choosing, decisions
ask and tell

learn about our
bodies changing
grow

WE

don't ever do
reasons addicted

use our brains
know whose job it is

not too often
moderation

WE

friends
getting on with people
feelings persuaders

work out the risks
uncertain

active outdoors relax
excercise heart

hazards
dangers opinions
facts drugs
alcohol A.I.D.S.

lifestyles different
admire copy respect
review advertising change
contract

A class of mixed ability eleven year olds, starting a new topic, offered these ideas which their teacher clustered in a circle formation.

In the topic work which followed, the children developed the themes in scientific terms and as aspects of health and personal and social education. They displayed this circle of ideas, key concepts and vocabulary, and used it as a plan and guideline for their topic work.

New ideas and vocabulary were collected as the topic progressed.

Remember the Circle of Feelings you used before? You could adapt this activity to use with children to explore their own and other's feelings.

You will have encouraged the children to put their feelings into words, to search for the exact words that describe what and how they feel. You will, in doing all this, have helped them to extend the language of their feelings and to use it appropriately, so that sharing and telling becomes easier.

WHAT WAS THAT ALL ABOUT?

We started by looking at circles as a valuable means of communication. We then concentrated on specific uses of the circle for communication.

We started with People Circles and looked at ways in which issues are more easily dealt with when everybody has an equal voice.

We then moved to Circles of Feelings and looked at these as vehicles for discussion, reflection, understanding and evaluation. We moved on to describe ways in which these Circles of Feelings can be recorded and become a valuable method of exploring other areas of the curriculum.

This led us to look at the use of Word Circles as a strategy for collecting ideas, opinions, views, reactions and feelings, and the way in which this structure can help individual work to blossom from a shared starting point.

Reflections

In the last section we mentioned the importance of helping children to reflect on their feelings, and to share them.

Some children may find it difficult to come and tell you face to face how they are feeling. Feelings of delight may be easier to express, so that interrupting a busy adult to share some cause for celebration is acceptable and not threatening. To interrupt with concerns, fears or unresolved problems takes much more - perhaps too much - doing. You may be able to set up with your class some code which means"I need to talk to you, soon, without everyone else being around".

One teacher uses

"Miss Yaxley, can I have two minutes?"

for her children to signal a need to talk.

You could encourage children to use writing as a way of reflecting on their feelings and sharing them with you.

An early way-in would be to provide each child with a book, which could be titled *In My Head.* Invite the children to use these books to record in writing, drawing, or a combination of both, some of their feelings, thoughts, hopes, ideas, plans, concerns, setting them out in any way they wish, including circles of feelings.

It would be fun to make your own In My Head Book to share with the children. Not all children will want, or feel ready, to do this, so it is important to make it optional. Remind them that this is a confidential activity, shared only with you as and when they decide. If you can find recycled envelopes into which the children put their books for delivery and return you will reinforce this confidentiality.

Children who are not yet independent writers will need to know that you will act as scribe for them and talk with them about what is in their heads.

Children who are becoming independent writers may prefer to bring their books to you and share what they have written. You could then offer to act as scribe to complete what they want to tell you.

Others may prefer to write it all themselves and leave their books in a special place, tray or box, knowing that only you will read what they have written and will be sure to respond.

At every stage the children will be rewarded and confidentiality boosted when you make it a two-way correspondence, with notes, messages and personal comments.

A useful addition would be a feelings wordbox displayed on the classroom wall. Here the children could share in building up words and phrases describing their feelings.

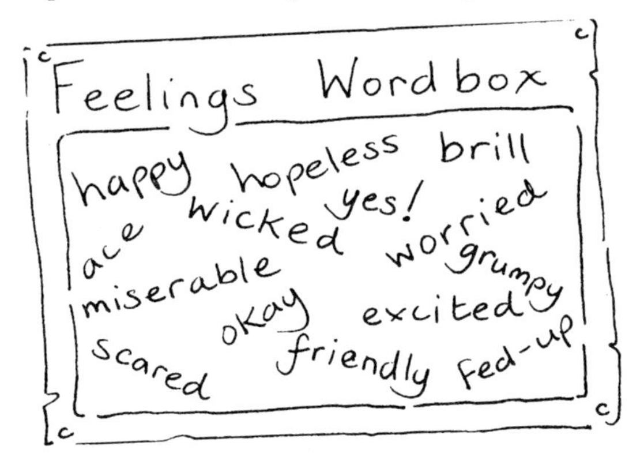

Once this idea has been introduced it is easy to develop it further by introducing "*Think Books*" or "*Journals*". Children who may feel shy or who lack the confidence to explore issues and feelings openly with you can use these notebooks as a private channel of communication. Children who feel that there is no time or space in their or your busy day to share feelings and concerns can use them too. Children who feel that their concerns take priority over everyone else's and think that your time is entirely theirs can also be encouraged to use this channel of communication.

Remind the children to re-read their think books to themselves now and then and to find the concerns or problems which have been resolved. Remind them to look for pleasures, delights, hopes and plans which were all the better for being shared in this way.

Ground rules for activities such as these might have already been established, but they need to be made very clear at this stage.

"Anything which you write in this book will be confidential between you and me, your teacher, and I will try to respond quickly. You could write about things you feel pleased about, the way you feel about the present and the future, worries you might have about schoolwork, friendships, growing up or problems at home and school, anything that you would like to share."

A caveat has to be given to the children however, that some issues cannot remain confidential and that if these extremes are reached it will be assumed that the writer wants to share the problem and is asking to be helped. In these circumstances, after discussion with the child, the appropriate course of action would be taken.

There should also be the opportunity to write something which explores thoughts which are not for sharing but need to be articulated. A flap of paper stuck over something and marked "Private" would, of course, need to be respected. Don't worry if some children don't make use of the books: they will manage to find your ear if they need to, and if you make it available.

You may find that some children are reluctant to use writing as a means of sharing their feelings with you. Some of that reluctance may stem from the struggle the children are having with the difficult process of becoming a writer. Their feelings and the need to share them may be very strong but the task of capturing those feelings in writing may seem impossible. In particular they may have concerns about the importance in this situation of correct spelling and presentation. You will need to convey to these children the level of importance you attach to correct writing in this particular situation, and to reiterate that this is a private form of communication.

Whatever strategy you choose to encourage the children to reflect on their feelings, to talk and write about them, to share them, you can be certain that you are helping them to feel good about themselves.

You will have demonstrated that their feelings are important to you and that you want to share them. You will have given the children public and private ways of articulating their feelings so that they get better at understanding them. You will have encouraged the children to celebrate some of their feelings and to cope with others. You will have helped them to see that other people, children and adults, experience the same kind of feelings, concerns, delights and fears.

Reflecting on the Day

How often are our children asked, on returning home from school, "What did you do at school today?"

or more specifically

"*What did you learn at school today?*"

How often do our children take refuge in answers such as

"*I can't remember*"

"*Lots of things*"

"*Nothing much*"

"*We played and had dinner and a story and then we came home*"

It may be that the children have been so involved in the day's activities that they find it difficult to recall all that has happened during a day in school, even more difficult to recall the day in sequence. So, they may pick out a few good or bad 'memorable' moments, which do nothing to reassure them or the parent that learning is taking place.

For most children, an enjoyable activity, especially if it has a fun name, or has been called a game by the teacher, can't be described at home as 'work' - it was too much fun.

So, some time taken to reflect upon the day's activities and to discover the learning that has taken place will help to provide some answers to the dreaded tea-time question.

BUT DIDN'T YOU DO ANY WORK?

The children may only need this few minutes at the end of a day or part of a day in order to look back and reflect on what has been asked of them and how well they have done and what they feel good about.

It's not so much -"Who has finished this piece of work, or got this all correct, or done the best piece of writing, painted the best picture?" It is more about the thought and effort which has gone into the doing, the having to share, wait, start again, change course, try a new skill, revise an old one. How can we find time to do this when every minute is precious, when children often feel they must hurry to get things done, when suddenly the bell rings and it's time to go home? Here are some ideas you might use to help all children to see their individual contributions as a positive part of the whole day, which also make clear the way in which the whole day has contributed to each child's learning. These ideas all demand that you put aside a few of the day's precious minutes but there are rewards which can go beyond all expectations when you build a period of reflection into the children's day.

Reflecting on the day as a class

Try to set aside a time at the end of the day to talk together, to run through the shared activities, the comings and goings, the quiet moments, the noisy ones which ended in laughter or tears. This review is one in which all, including you, can take part, where successes can be shared, failures put into perspective, new directions planned.

At first you may want to keep the review very general, reflecting together on all that the class as a whole has tackled and achieved, discovered, learned, and enjoyed. You could invite the children to summarise the day, perhaps using a wordbox which they have helped to devise and to which they add new vocabulary.

Reflecting on the day in more personal ways

When working as a class you could begin to reflect on the day through other frameworks, focussing on the processes rather than on specific outcomes. Each of the frameworks suggested below provides the children with positive ways of reflecting on their own progress and learning, and on their individual contributions to the day.

Five Ways of Looking Back

This framework offers the children five simple questions to answer as a structure for reviewing their days. Starting with:

Who has done something today they've never done before?

If there is time you could invite the children to share their experiences with the class, a group, or a partner If not, a show of hands can be a quick reward. Don't forget to put your own hand up to share your "Never before" experience - if you have had one.

It is important that the children realise that they cannot expect to do something new every day. At the same time you can encourage them to think in small terms, to recognise each small step as progress. Encourage them, too, to think in terms of relationships in and out of the classroom, to realise that small gestures of friendship, small steps towards greater independence or tolerance are important, and to share these.

You then go on to ask:

Who has done something better today than they've done before?

Again it would be good to share, but a show of hands, a quick count up and a general praising is rewarding.

Some children may be reluctant to praise themselves, or be unaware that they have done things better than before. You will want to be able to pick up this reluctance, and to help these children by reminding them of the progress you have seen them making.

Next, you ask:

Who has done something today and it has gone all wrong?

If there is time, invite the children to share these experiences and to say how they dealt with them. Your own admission of failure could be important here. The children will have the opportunity of seeing that other people fail and can say so, can put failure behind them, and even laugh at it sometimes.

Your last two questions focus on helping and being helped:

Who has helped somebody today?

You could hope that every child would signify being a helper. Some children may not see themselves in this way so you may be able to point out a moment in the day when they helped you or you observed them being helpful. This would be a good moment to put up your own hand (or both hands).

Who has been helped by somebody else today?

Your own hand could be the first to be raised, reminding children that to need help and find it is a positive experience, and doesn't suggest incompetence, stupidity, or lack of skill.

You might end by suggesting that the children roll up their five-fold reflection of the day and take it home in their heads or on paper. So when someone at home asks "Well - what have you done at school today?" the child can then unroll the reflection and share it.

Which hats have you worn today?

Reflections on the day through this framework could begin by talking with the children about all the rôles played by them during a day. You could help them to reflect through this framework by devising a chart illustrating the many different rôles children can take on in one day. You could illustrate the chart yourself, or ask the children to find or draw the pictures. You can adapt the language and number of possible hats as appropriate to the children.

You might like to choose from some of the following, simplifying the vocabulary where necessary:

actor
artist
athlete
author
computer operator
dancer
designer
detective
embellisher
engineer
exhibitor
expert
fairtester
geographer
gymnast
historian
interviewer
investigator
listener
mathematician
musician
observer
painter
pastrycook
player
poet
reader
recorder
reporter
researcher
reviewer
scientist
speaker
technician
visitor
writer

Children might like the opportunity to make and take home a written or pictorial record of the different rôles they have played in one day. It might be useful to warn them that they may be asked to substantiate their claims to being scientists or authors, for example, and to be prepared for challenges such as "A scientist! When were you a scientist? What kind of science were you doing?"

How have you worked today?

This framework provides the children with a different way of reviewing the day. It involves focussing on all the ways it is possible to work in the classroom. You could invite the children to respond to questions such as "*Who has worked alone today? With a partner? With a group? With the whole class? With one grown-up? With people you chose? With people you didn't choose? With people you know? With people you didn't know?*"

This could lead to a discussion of being, at different times, a leader, an organiser, a helper, a starter of new things, a finisher, a repairer. You could develop, if there is time, some further reflections on rules and relationships both in and out of the classroom.

What have you learned to do today?

This framework focuses on skills and asks the children to identify new skills which they have been tackling and old skills which they have been practising or extending. It also asks the children to identify some skills which still require some time spent on them. This framework is particularly useful when the children have been working in groups, exploring aspects of a topic or a theme.

One class of nine year olds used it as a way of reflecting on the progress of their topic work.

Home grown frameworks

You could develop your own frameworks for reflecting, whether on a day, a week, or a topic. For instance, you might decide to focus the reflection on reading, asking the children to think of and record in some way, possibly through you, all the different types of material they have been reading. You will find that, once the children begin to look back, they have been reading a wide variety of materials. These will include their own writing, other people's writing, wall displays, notices, instructions, printed books and papers of all kinds. You might also ask the children to try to recall not only what they read, but when, where, why and to whom. You and they could devise ways of recording this information and making it something to take home at the end of the day.

Remind the children that when they get home, they may be asked questions about their day at school, what they did, what they learned. Suggest that they surprise those asking by telling them far more than they expect to hear. You may find that not only does this help the child to feel good, it can also make the parents and families feel good too.

WHAT WAS THAT ALL ABOUT?

We said that children need to be helped to reflect on their days, to see, in positive terms, the processes of the day and their contribution to the day itself. We developed the idea of Journal writing for younger children and explained how it can be used with older age groups to help children articulate their feelings, and how important this articulation is in helping people feel good about themselves.

We have emphasised this, rather than focussing on getting the right answers or doing the best piece of work, as the important things.

We have accepted that it takes valuable time, time you may be reluctant to give away, but have set out to show how important and productive it is in terms of feeling good, of knowing you are learning, and being able to tell others about it.

We have suggested a range of frameworks for looking back through the day and for enabling the children to answer the questions "What did you do?" and "What did you learn in school today?" in ways which make them and those asking the questions feel good.

Conclusion

What Else Can we Say?

We started by saying that this was not another National Curriculum book, but that it was about something which was more important. We hope that you have come some way to agreeing with us, to see that it is much more a practical book, a book about positive classroom life, about you, the children, their families, your colleagues and all those people who contribute to your classroom life. It's about all of you feeling good about what you are doing and trying to do.

We started by asking you to look at yourself, and feel good about yourself. Next, we looked at helping all the other people in your school community to feel good too. We looked at the ways in which we can use language to raise people's self-esteem rather than lower it. We looked at the importance of names and the deep significance they have for their owners. We looked at the use of circles as a way of removing barriers to communication, and finally we suggested a variety of approaches for reflecting on what has been achieved. If we put all that together, what will we have?

We will have schools, teachers, children, families feeling good about what they are achieving, feeling good about themselves. Not every day, but most of the time. If we have that, then we can do anything - what we believe in, as well as what is required of us.

But it doesn't just happen. It needs people who believe it can happen, who are prepared to try it. It needs people who know that it takes time, that it needs a whole school policy, supported by all who work in the school, regularly or occasionally. It needs to be a policy shared and understood by parents, families, governors, the community.

A tall order, but it can begin now in your classroom. Now is the time to start. First with yourself, then with your children then maybe with your colleagues and the whole school.

A school which promotes positive ways of feeling good will be a school which promotes education in its truest sense.

OTHER BOOKS BY NOREEN WETTON

health
for life
a guide for health
promoting schools

Written with Jenny McWhirter

This new book is an atlas of opportunity for teachers and heads in primary schools, and also for health education officers and advisers. From their wide experience gained through running training courses for thousands of teachers on the *PHIPS* and *Best of Health* projects, Noreen Wetton and Jenny McWhirter have written this guide to support teachers who want their schools to become active health promoting schools. Linking closely with the *Health for Life* materials, the book emphasises the importance of a carefully prepared health education curriculum and demonstrates how it may best be achieved through training, planning and use of sound techniques. The guide is accessible, full of ideas and inspirations, and a really practical starting point on the route to a health promoting school. If you are serious about including health education in your school's curriculum, this book is essential reading.

ISBN 0 901762 98 9 Price £10.50 (+ £1.95 p&p per order)

The Good Health Project Set 4

Written with Jenny McWhirter

This volume in this popular series contains teacher's notes and pupil worksheets to accompany the latest programmes in the Channel 4 Schools Good Health Series.
Contains: It's up to you; All around us; Smokebusters; Kieran; *and* Who do you think you are?

ISBN 0 901762 94 6 Price £10.50 (+ £1.95 p&p per order)